"'Souls of poets dead and gone,' goes the line from Keats, but A.J. Rathbun's wonderful *In Their Cups* brings them back, at least for a few more drinks, and we too are invited in. And what company we enjoy: we can imagine classic poets as diverse as Catullus and Du Fu speaking to polar opposite modernists like Cesare Pavese and Apollinaire, perhaps interrupted here and there by diverse contemporary voices such as Mark Halliday and William Olsen. Rathbun has created a unique imaginary world here, adding a couple of his own fine poems to the conversation, where we can hear, with Richard Hugo, the 'dusty jukebox cracking' on every page. This is a book you'll want to raise a glass to."

> —Richard Jackson, author of *Resonance* and
> *Unauthorized Autobiography: New and Selected Poems*

D1206393

In Their Cups

Edited by
A.J. Rathbun

*An anthology
of poems about*
**Drinking Places,
Drinks,
and Drinkers**

THE HARVARD COMMON PRESS | BOSTON, MASSACHUSETTS

The
Harvard
Common
Press
535
Albany
Street
Boston
Massachusetts
02118

www.harvardcommonpress.com

Copyright © 2010 by A.J. Rathbun

Printed in the United States of America
Printed on acid-free paper

Library of Congress Cataloging-in-Publication Data
In their cups : an anthology of poems about drinking
places, drinks, and drinkers / edited by A.J. Rathbun.
p. cm.
ISBN 978-1-55832-666-8 (pbk. : acid-free paper)
1. Drinking of alcoholic beverages—Poetry. 2. Bars (Drinking
establishments)—Poetry. I. Rathbun, A. J. (Arthur John), 1969–
PN6110.D85I5 2010
821'.00803564—dc22   2010009736

Special bulk-order discounts are available on this and
other Harvard Common Press books. Companies and
organizations may purchase books for premiums or
resale, or may arrange a custom edition, by contacting
the Marketing Director at the address above.

Book design by John Kramer Design
Cover photograph by Michael Hoy
Author photograph by Natalie Fuller

10   9   8   7   6   5   4   3   2   1

For my wondrous poetry teachers, who are also wonderful poets and who all also like a good drink: Elizabeth Dodd, William Olsen, Nancy Eimers, and Mark Halliday

CONTENTS

Drinks, Quaffs, and Consumables

Drinkers, Revelers, and Imbibers

ACKNOWLEDGMENTS

PUTTING TOGETHER A COLLECTION OF DRINKING POEMS IS, as you might expect, amazingly fun (it's two great things that go great together), but also a bit of work. I certainly couldn't have done it alone, and there are a whole epic's worth of thanks to go around. But if I wrote the full epic of thanks here, it would take time away from reading the poems that follow, and also take time away from shaking the drinks to be had while reading them, so I'll just focus on a few key thank-yous (more than a haiku's worth, but less than the epic).

First, a huge thanks to my editor Valerie Cimino (the Whitman of editors), helpful, fun, encouraging, and ready to delve into new projects without fear. Also, big thanks to all of the poetic folks at The Harvard Common Press, especially Pat Jalbert-Levine for going the extra stanzas in getting this done, and publisher Bruce Shaw for believing me when I said a collection of poems about drinking, drinkers, and drinks was a good idea (I suppose that extra bottle of wine we had didn't hurt, either).

A huge thanks also to my agent Michael Bourret (the Wordsworth of agents), for his relentless help, for the coaching, the fantastic support, the drinks, and the ability to add tranquility to any day that seems about to fly off its hinges. And for that matter, thanks to his partner Miguel, too, for the drinks and advice and for coming along with Michael when his clients drag him out to bars.

To go through and list every poet and teacher and translator who taught me something via their poems or conversations would be a worthy thing to do, but would take (as mentioned) a bit too long, as long probably as listing every bartender who ever made me a good drink. But a little extra mention is demanded for all those who have poems in the following pages. Wherever you are, thanks a bunch for allowing me to use your work, for writing such fantastic poems, and for continuing to make the world better. If we're ever in a bar together (in this world or any other) the next round's on me.

An even larger and more specific thanks must be delivered, however, to my pal the poet Ed Skoog. Ed, thanks for loaning me all the books, for standing in the kitchen sipping drinks and talking about how this book could come together, for continual support, for translating (wonderfully) poems at the drop of a poetic hat, and for being the smartest poet and writer I'll ever know. Having someone like you for a friend makes every second spent together worthwhile (even when, maybe especially when, you take me in one afternoon to every bar Richard Hugo ever visited in White Center).

A short stanza of thanks also go to a few folks who helped much in various ways when I was putting this collection together, including Brad P for bitters and support, Lisa Ekus and the Ekus crew for charm and always being ready to help, video director Dr. Gonzo and the Gonzo family, Leslie P and Mark B for web and biz advice, everyone in Ballard who buys me drinks (especially Jeremy Holt, Megan, and BB, who also provide veggie-friendly snacks), the folks who read and comment and come by my Spiked Punch blog at www.ajrathbun.com/blog (especially pal Philip who comes for the comic references, but stays for the drinks), and my family near and far (with a giant line of thanks to my parents, Art and Trudy, and stepmother Teresa, who encouraged the poetry in me from the start). Oh, an almost last line of thanks to you, too, for supporting poetry and good drinks.

But the last line of thanks goes of course to my closest family, my wife Natalie (along with a sideways shout-out to the world's most poetic dogs, Sookie and Rory), who never hesitated to help when I said "hey, I want to put out a literary magazine, and maybe publish some books of poems" and never blinked when I said "well, I think I want to write about drinks now, too." Thanks doll, for always backing me in my various and sundry endeavors, for not caring when the books of poems and drinks strain the bookshelves, and for understanding that art in all its forms is worthwhile and worth supporting. *Il mio amore per voi è l'amore che sposta il sole e tutte le altre stele.*

THE TWENTY-FIRST-CENTURY DRINKING REVOLUTION IS IN full swing, and people are devoting more and more time to sipping on chilly cocktails at home and in the bar, as well as sharing more glasses of good wine and beer with friends on the veranda, hooting it up with a couple highballs and pals on the back porch, and sipping digestifs in the den with dear ones after dinner. Although moments like these are singular and individual, they mirror past moments and, in so doing, become a part of a larger legacy: the legacy of folks who enjoy a drink with others, who laugh and sing and whisper with glass in hand.

The fact is that these moments tend to be memorable and full of life. This has led to a desire to have appropriate words to match up with these occasions, which is a natural desire, as communication through language is one of the things that makes us human. Conversing at the bar (be it a home or out-of-home bar) may be said to be even livelier than at other places, as a good drink loosens the tongue, enthralls the mind, and increases the craving for communication. This is why drinkers and revelers have gravitated so readily to poetry, and why a large number of poets, by nature devoted to living life intensely, have written and continue to write poems about bars, drinks, and drinkers.

This collection in your hands follows that vision, as it contains a wide range of drinking poems, works that range from classics to freshly minted marvels that will rapidly become favorites. It's like a cocktail party where poets from throughout the centuries gather around the bar to spin stories, odes, songs, sorrows, and happiness, surrounded by bottles, ice, you, and your friends. It's a literate affair, but one that's inclusive and enjoyable and never stuffy or staid. Like the best parties, there are some rollicking numbers and some folks who may have had a glass too many. There are also those in love and those celebrating life at the top of their voices, those thinking seriously about their subject, those who are on an early round, and those who know it might just be their last sip. It's a place where all are welcome, a place you'll want to inhabit with friends, reading out loud and toasting and making drinks the whole time.

I've been lucky to have spent a fair amount of time with poets in bars and with poetic bartenders, both those who get paid for their shaking and those whose currency is being known as a fantastic party thrower. Through these friendships and friends, and through those I've made with a drink in one hand and a book in the other, I've found out how well verse and good drinks go together (rather like bourbon and bitters). Both are driven by a love of balance and good taste, while at the same time being open to wild fits of imagination and of worldly things. As poets and bartenders are both natural storytellers, there is yet another level of interconnectedness between the two disciplines.

That isn't the main reason for this collection, but it is why there are many fantastic poems about bars, drinks, and drinkers (and though I feel those in the following pages are choice companions, there are many more out there waiting for you to read them). No, the real reason for this collection is because with the renewed emphasis on well-made cocktails and good wines and beers, all consumed with those close to us, there is a deep need for a collection of poems to provide imbibers both with something to read that celebrates the activity they're taking part in as well as providing a language to regale fellow drinkers with—giving you something to show friends and family and something to read out loud to them while enjoying the very drinks and bars (or bars much like those inside) celebrated in this book. Basically, I believe the poems in this book make the world (at least the world of the bar) a better place. And that's something worth writing a poem about.

Bars, Taverns, and Inns

"All bars are snug places, but the Maypole's was the very snuggest, cosiest, and completest bar, that ever the wit of man devised. Such amazing bottles in old oaken pigeon-holes; such gleaming tankards dangling from pegs at about the same inclination as thirsty men would hold them to their lips; such sturdy little Dutch kegs ranged in rows on shelves . . ."

— Charles Dickens, *Barnaby Rudge*

Lines on the Mermaid Tavern

Souls of Poets dead and gone,
What Elysium have ye known,
Happy field or mossy cavern,
Choicer than the Mermaid Tavern?
Have ye tippled drink more fine
Than mine host's Canary wine?
Or are fruits of Paradise
Sweeter than those dainty pies
Of venison? O generous food!
Drest as though bold Robin Hood
Would, with his maid Marian,
Sup and bowse from horn and can.

I have heard that on a day
Mine host's sign-board flew away,
Nobody knew whither, till
An astrologer's old quill
To a sheepskin gave the story,
Said he saw you in your glory,
Underneath a new old-sign

Sipping beverage divine,
And pledging with contented smack
The Mermaid in the Zodiac.

Souls of Poets dead and gone,
What Elysium have ye known,
Happy field or mossy cavern,
Choicer than the Mermaid Tavern?

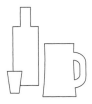

The Last Round at the Index Tavern

> *Eat, drink, and be fat and drunk*
> —button advertising the Index Tavern

Outside, the tin 1950s Squirt sign stands
fifteen feet tall in the sun. Salmon
run the Cascades into our various
valleys while the pharmacist buries
Guinness and the bearded ex-hippies now

out-of-work loggers untap High Life's
and sway relentlessly to 1980s Brit-pop.
Sheila take a, Sheila take a bow. Do you
really want to hurt me carved in the Men's
below *to hell with Sultan* and above *regret.*

We pay off our debts and don't sleep apart,
Manhattans and bass and the Skykomish roll
our personal roulette, tuck us
into bruised beds where a scratchy Marlene
Dietrich movie plays, in which we kiss

but don't exactly make up. Air the door
to any good bar at least one more time.
Sit smoking afternoon into swollen evening
and count Subarus, Saturns, Fords, Chevrolets.
The equation is complex. Back out of Index's

three endings—evidence, a wedding, thirteen
words that echo off Osprey—and spill
into the bartender's sleeves. Without dust,
luck, or elk to follow, everyone leaves
an empty room, a barstool, a last swallow.

Fragmentia: On Honorable Life

*Live a good and honorable life. Then, when
you get older and thir—*

excuse me, *thirsty,* you can drive
your life, weak but well-dressed
to the nearest watering hole
and trade it in for a cold pitcher.

It's a real life, you tell the barkeep,
you can bite it yourself. But this causes
problems because the bartender does
and as his horse's teeth sink in, your life,
both good and honorable, cries out,
"Kind sir!" and slaps the barkeep
with a lavender glove.

                    Then
the duel out back in the dusty alley
and the abandoned pitcher growing warm
on the bar and the search for seconds, what
can you do but agree, you'd be a lout
to slink off.

　　　　　　And they're back to back now
and striding and the barkeep, knowing better
than to promise to be anything but alive,
is turning early, his pistol improbably large
and black, and he's blowing away your life,

which, good and honorable, hits his knees
still counting, his face bewildered
by all that has come after 8, an infinity
of numbers, all turning away, shuffling off,
kicking the dirt, going back inside,
where it's cool and the world is waiting.

Missouri Bar

In Missouri there must be this bar
where the real other life transpires. It is
so real. It is not exotic; instead it exposes
the illusion of the exotic by being at once so
ordinary and so textured. For the folks drinking there
this bar is a place near home and just a bar
except it is extra real in this dense easy way
lubricated by alcohol, but for me it is so much
where I am not. What if I could walk in there
and discover the thousand non-clichés there

in that blue-shady half-dark among those Missouri drinkers
some bitter some itchy with loneliness some with comic lust
all this very solid while also spiced:
several speak of bets placed on horses, boxers, drivers—
detail is lavish fueled by knowledge,
these people are not stupid, I realize now
this lack of stupidity does distinguish this one bar
which is not exotic but *extra* real,
they speak of what is what
from right smack in it—what if I could hear them
and not miss everything? "Shaver's boy took that pedal-steel
and put guts in his daddy's tunes"

"Old Brankin lost that thousand last August
gon' be poppin' clutch to jump out front of Cedric and them
come Tuesdee" "and him still saying vagrant rhymes with fragrant"
I am not quite catching
"Marbella said you don't got the check
you don't bring TJ for his good time Saturday"
"buck naked on Sunday" they are not stupid, they are so
fully *in* it
              hence the talk lavish as in "rich" novels
but this more something than any novel, more crunky
more crunkydunk than any novel
but me not catching it—

what would it be for me if I did? Me there
at a table with such a discreet small black notebook,
nobody notices it, they just don't, they're all around me
like this big man in a blue baseball cap, the insignia is
either of a pro team or an electricians' union,
he leans toward me on un-shy reddened elbows telling
how the mayor tried to catch the police chief selling cocaine,
another guy tells tales of a poker game where you need a knife
and each player has a witty odd nickname, or not,
I'm not sure, but I find out when I'm there
and it's not clichés, also the story of how Robbie met Marge
at the crafts fair—

                    this is making me tired but
when I'm there I'm not tired at all
hearing all about someone's sarcastic sister
and the frustration of certain sexual hopes at Evelyn's Diner,
all unstupid and true in the grainy way

while in my unseen black notebook I write it down
losing none of it, and Charlotte doesn't notice
nor does the man who is half Pawnee.
Hours and hours I'm there not impatiently,
never wishing I was reading instead.
Brad who knows everything about refrigerators,
his second divorce; Lillian whose twin sons are in the Air Force
on Guam. "Guam" I say, nodding in sympathy which is real,
I know both laughter and tears, I finish six beers

till it is only the natural inevitable
when Darlene or Colinda comes to my table in her tight jeans,
not exotic, just so fully actual, stands close to me,
I can see she is forty and has had forty men
and I want her, Colinda of embodied knowledge
who says "Watchin' golf on TV is not my idea of a big weekend"
and her hand touches my wrist so matter-of-factly,
"We can say we're sorry tomorrow"—she has thus
made my wrist part of what is available in Missouri

so plainly she can connect me including my wakened cock
for which she has three funny names
to what is
　　　　so I shove the black notebook into my back pocket
and walk with Darlene out to her car
which is a big horsey 1973 something—
in the front seat I'm throbbing but amazingly at peace
(with the notebook bent under my buttock)
because at last I'm going to be *there*
at the worn tough dark heart of
Missouri
and it must mean—or just be—something deep so deep.

Half Ghosts

In the flux of this bar, regulars come and go, shifting like
    constellations,
shapes changed but always similar darkness
in between the illuminated points. What makes anyone return?
Suggested answer: They want something from you, the bartender,
    seek a connection,
an appeasement of a swollen void. Of ghosts, parapsychologists
    theorize the same:
until a festering desire is soothed, spirits continue to haunt.

***

Pocono Bob, nick-named so because he commutes to the city from
    the Poconos,
tells me ghost stories, translucent cheekbones framed in a window,
a phantom yellow Labrador, and his first wife, who died in his
    arms.
The keg I'm pulling his pints from kicks. To change it,
I descend to the basement. Down here, there are ghosts,
    fantasmas,
according to the kitchen guys, so I flick my eyeballs into dank
    corners
expecting a misty torso, a frosted glow, a severed stiletto encasing
    a foot.

There are thousands of reasons for ghosts to live here, and though
     I feel
a vulnerable space at the base of my neck, like living
in a tent on a flood plain, this time, I see nothing.

Back upstairs, Pocono Bob has abandoned ghosts
for his beloved subject, again, Susan, the stimulant snorter, thirty
     years his junior.
This time she's stolen a couple of his guns. Last week, he found her
     limping
along the woods-lined road, blond hair brown, beat up, pale face
     yellow-blue-black, high,
hazel eyes red, all the shades she shouldn't be. In the flux, what
     makes someone return?
They return because we allow them to, we encourage them to
     come back.
We want to be what's sought after.

***

Sometimes I wouldn't see Pocono Bob for days and I'd dread he'd
     died alone
in his big Pennsylvania home, shot in the chest by one of Susan's
     drunk boyfriends.
Then, sure as a sliver of moon after the new moon, he'd return as if
     he'd never left—

been sick or *iced in*—he'd say. Pocono Bob took severance when
  Merrill Lynch consolidated.
It's been six months. When a regular stops returning, it echoes
  death. A layer of a life added
to the history of the bar like a layer of paint on an old wall. They
  become a half ghost, not dead (or maybe
dead), always here because they were always here. And if Pocono
  Bob returns, it will be like he never left.
I'll pour him his drink, my hand tilting the bottle, grabbing it first
  by the neck.

The White Hart

—for Jaime Curl, somewhere over the Atlantic

I thought I'd left off scribbling about bars
for the dignity of the lone figure just now
hauling another creel into a gently bobbing skiff
a half mile out past the seawall.
But when I think of the grace we seek
it's the smile on the carved corbel
in the oldest inn in Edinburgh,
ceiling beam atop his head, noose around his neck,
that comes to me. Is that smile
knowing gallows long gone from Grassmarket out front
or ignorance of the rope some grim-humored innkeep
added for the tourists? Respite and ignorance
are minor graces but the portrait of Burns
above the fire didn't seem to mind.
Half of last night's living pub
were Ireland supporters in for the rugby
and cheap pound. No matter if they sang
"Dirty Old Town" thinking Dublin or if Scotland
had to lose when their team won;
it's the grace of places we leave not to remember us.
That those places don't remember us

is our grace too, if we'll take it.
We're gone with last week's sunset on waves
pushing in to the rock beach below Duntulm ruins,
gone from wind flattening grass on a Skye ridgeline,
gone from the White Hart with five centuries
of minor grace seekers and sing-alongers before us.
That smiling figurehead has sailed
his noose and ceiling-beam bowsprit beyond us.
To the Celts, a white hart meant the unattainable.
Since David King of Scotland prayed God
to spare him from a white hart's charge
and God answered with a cross in the antlers,
the white hart's meant luck to the Scots.
Luck's yet another minor grace in amber
between "The Skye Boat Song" and "Loch Lamond"
while we sang maudlin loud and read the past
on the lips of the old, ruddy man sitting underwater
under the corbel. On the corbel sailed
and smiled, without so much as a flinch
at the bombs from 1916's zeppelin
or wink when the Irish lass left
her kiss on your American cheek and her straw
in the dregs of a long-neck Bud.
I thought I'd left off scribbling about bars,

but when I look up from the desk, figure,
skiff and creel have taken their dignity elsewhere.
Grace. You've left your word
like a brass coin on beer-wet wood.
Alone beside my mid-day cottage fire
I smile grace to the empty sea.

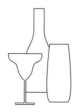

The White Rose Over the Water

The old men sat with hats pull'd down,
    Their claret cups before them:
Broad shadows hid their sullen eyes,
    The tavern lamps shone o'er them,
As a brimming bowl, with crystal fill'd,
    Came borne by the landlord's daughter,
Who wore in her bosom the fair white rose,
    That grew best over the water.

Then all leap'd up, and join'd their hands
    With hearty clasp and greeting,
The brimming cups, outstretch'd by all,
    Over the wide bowl meeting.
"A health," they cried, "to the witching eyes
    Of Kate, the landlord's daughter!
But don't forget the white, white rose
    That grows best over the water."

Each others' cups they touch'd all round,
    The last red drop outpouring;
Then with a cry that warm'd the blood,
    One heart-born chorus roaring—

"Let the glass go round, to pretty Kate,
   The landlord's black-eyed daughter;
But never forget the white, white rose
   That grows best over the water."

Then hats flew up and swords sprang out,
   And lusty rang the chorus—
"Never," they cried, "while Scots are Scots,
   And the broad Frith's before us."
A ruby ring the glasses shine
   As they toast the landlord's daughter,
Because she wore the white, white rose
   That grew best over the water.

A poet cried, "Our thistle's brave,
   With all its stings and prickles;
The shamrock with its holy leaf
   Is spar'd by Irish sickles.
But bumpers round, for what are these
   To Kate, the landlord's daughter,
Who wears at her bosom the rose as white,
   That grows best over the water?"

They dash'd the glasses at the wall,
    No lip might touch them after;
The toast had sanctified the cups
    That smash'd against the rafter;
Then chairs thrown back, they up again
    To toast the landlord's daughter,
But never forgot the white, white rose
    That grew best over the water.

The-Way-We-Were Lounge

This is the kind of place I loved when I walked
across Italy looking every night for open
spaces. I would have lain on my back
staring up at the two rusty cedar trees
and the broken notes and the tilted cocktail glass.
I would have sung myself to sleep
thinking about Padua and little Verona with the rose walls.
I was like a gorilla, making a new
bed every night, digging a hole so I could
lie on the ground without breaking my bones.
I was a believer—the one time in my life—
traveling from town to town with my marble notebook
full of dark signs and incantations.
I would have loved the swaying pole
and the white sidewalk.
I would have waited for hours
to put my shoes on
and wash my face at the iron spigot.
I would have stood up like a devout shadow
to look at the moon again in the first daylight.

The Dead Monkey

A face framed in a pink lace baby's hood was youth and age
collapsed to a wizened black walnut. It had no idea
that we were there, New Orleans, 1981, or that we were
growing envious of its owner, an unshaven but rich-looking
    Mexican
who hoisted it from the ground, not altogether modest
about the attention he and it were getting from all of us,
eating our beignets, watching this binary configuration,
man and monkey, kiss, kiss again, patching up
some make-believe quarrel between lovers.
Suddenly it leapt up a trellis of morning glory vines,
swung from a brass chandelier over the human circus of
    breakfasters
and scrambled across the street into a moving bus,
arms and legs toppling one over the other
as it tried to keep up with its death.
The man walked out to the ridiculous end to his happiness,
stealing the delight from us, like surreptitious newlyweds,
poor enough in spirit to be amazed by fact.
Taking it in his arms, crying to make himself alone,
this Mexican was living proof that suffering
is not all that crazy about company.
When the crowd dispersed, he seemed relieved,

as if too much had already been suffered
without us adding our thimbleful.
That night we saw the Mexican without his monkey in a bar,
buying everyone drinks and laughing hysterically
about the whole thing, saying *death is my life*.
If that sounds a bit dramatic, blame it
on sweet bourbon, this is just what he said,
being just lucid enough to mix up life and death
and stupid enough to want to share in their confusion.
We toasted with him to stupidity because
there's not always enough stupidity around to celebrate,
and when we were good and drunk we turned ourselves out
    into the night,
between more bars we saw more bars,
windows like photographs fleshed out with
bodies that destroyed their secrets,
we took the journey across the dangerous street,
entranced by the idea of getting somewhere,
sick for everything but home.

The Last Saturn Bar Poem

Around the art barn, Mike Frolich's bar-tab
bartered paintings hang the hell that rose with him
from the Gulf of Mexico floor too fast, torturing
blood with air: maniac fish, demon in a diving bell,
and then from cadmium sunset through marsh comes
the boat bearing forward in grand roving the name
O'Neal, our bartender. Theirs are the dreams we enter,
entering the Saturn Bar's owly heat re-tooled for unlovely
loss, the rattled corner leaning away from Chartreuse, neat,
and when I'm able to dream jukebox damaged warbling,
a Saturn-like-thing opens within me, but this is the last
Saturn Bar poem—I'll try, I'll try—to stop singing
shadows of St. Claude and Clouet on security camera
pavement grays we keep talking about with increasing
reluctance, ready to move on to fresh bewilderments,
spiraling neon, neon that lights up my nameless shot.

At the Tavern

A lilt and a swing,
And a ditty to sing,
Or ever the night grow old;
The wine is within,
And I'm sure 't were a sin
For a soldier to choose to be cold, my dear,
For a soldier to choose to be cold.

We're right for a spell,
But the fever is—well,
No thing to be braved, at least;
So bring me the wine;
No low fever in mine,
For a drink is more kind than a priest, my dear,
For a drink is more kind than a priest.

Meteorology Off Moclips

This empty tavern knows
wind again; stained chairs, the leaky
ceiling have nothing
on the way gusts off the Pacific
beat time with the season. Monday's sun becomes
a vest I wear Tuesday
when the seagull tracks turn to tortoises, the easy
edge of flippers divide
the sand and then
it is finished. Wednesday dives inside
out, answers my questions about anchors
and the sough of surf becomes unfinished bedtime rhymes.

Around the point the rocks
close in as lovers and I can't
hear for all the chatter. Out front, the road
clears its conscience and remains impassable
so I take to naming beer coasters and collecting
archetypes in hopes that in the shelter
I build here with blue hands and familiar
dances, I'll find the storm's lee.

Downstairs at the Garden of Allah

"Her body aches for one more man. The right man."
—Neile Graham, *St. Maudlin (La Folle)*

—Arlington Hotel, Seattle, WA, 1948

Punch-drunk tired after a day shift hauling
    freight on the docks, wages stuffed in my wallet,
I'm Friday-night flush, dressed to the nines,
    clean suit pressed and fresh rose in my lapel.
I brave the briny chill off Elliott Bay.
    Dodge winos palming their hooch in paper bags
beneath the totem pole in Pioneer Square.
    Those same Skid Row regulars Sister Faye and me
preached to before she run off, our Mission
    funds going straight in her veins.
I'm hounded by ferry horns along 1st Ave,
    sailors cruising to Rivoli Theatre burlesques.
Shivering on the corner a hooker hustles,
    come-ons for a cheap quick blow.
She tempts me while I shadowbox my urges.
    I'm thinking a beer, time to figure out what I want
would be nice when I spot the Arlington Hotel.
    Its marble archway. White stairs

down to the Garden of Allah. I fold a dollar bill
    through the ornate metal door's peephole.

Matron checks me out, nods me into this oasis,
    fake palm trees and stenciled stars on the walls.
Tacky tables and chairs packed tight, so I
    barely squeeze by brawny sailors three deep
at the bar. I shout my beer order, almost outdone
    by Wurlitzer blasts, by cat calls,
whistling as I twist around, see Jackie Starr
    grip the microphone hangs down from the ceiling above
center stage. No scenery distracts me
    taking in his sequined gown, flashy ermine wrap.
My Lauren Bacall. Jackie's one svelte player, a gal a man
    like me sure could go for: savvy, confident.
No 5 o'clock shadow, nothing gruff
    about her crooning *As Time Goes By*.
Made-up dandies and rough types
    swoon at big beautiful Vivien Leigh eyes, her
pearl necklace and earrings a-sparkle.
    Jackie'd command respect from harassing cops,
while less brassy dames fear
    a nightstick to the ribs, a ticket, jail time.

This dangerous charm, this perfect man.
    In the Garden of Allah everyone's nuts over her act.
I sneak a glance at two broads, not usuals
    at honky-tonks, private supper clubs below the line.
Whoever we are we are Jackie's crowd.
    She finishes, sits by me for a cigarette.
Lipstick rings around the filter tip.
    Her fingers slide over my hand, and I'm hers.
Those silk stockings caressing
    my pant leg, she leans in, smoothes my hair,
frees the rose. Plants it in her stylish
    auburn curls, so I notice. She's the real deal.
Her brazen slender hips tease, whisper.
    Their sway a pledge with each frothy gulp of my Rainier.
She saunters on stage down to a g-string,
    baiting the turned-on audience who busily model
themselves after her. In the song's
    misty glow I fancy Jackie lets that last bit
slip, tangled in our bed sheets, kissing.
Both of us crave the heady sweat on a man's skin.

Cocktail Lounge with Imagined Birdsong

My colleagues disassembled and downsized
each other's sense of self all day.
And the landscape out that window:
a tiny, well-planned, oily patch
of manicured, sturdy fescue wrapped
in transparent parking lot.
For today's debriefing, I'm drinking
straight up, getting productively slanted
at the holy end of the Apex bar
at the bottom of the Oakland Avenue hill
where the sun is turning over and every hour is happy.
The loneliest old man I've ever known,
who's sitting where he sits every day, has a theory.
Yeah, we say, and when the streetlamps
pop and hum and crackle before never flickering on,
it almost sounds like the song of a red-winged
    blackbird.
If I could stand, I might get up
and gaze through the bullet hole
in the fissured glass block window

and see what's left of midweek's ambitious light
slanting over a wormwood fence
cloaked with morning glories
in the littered empty lot across Clay,
and almost imagine an outline
of the blackbird as it sat chirping
perched on the edge
of a furrow of abject tires
until the sky would run out of time
and the great constellations
would push themselves into one another
composing some random ideas of order.

Assumptions

Only the plain girls stay in this town
where the quiet is so violent
that sidewalks seethe and pitch,
where wind will chasten a face.

Beyond yawning gates,
the church spire punctures
pure sky and transgressions
are never forgiven.

Flags snap to tatters along Main,
and only the tavern stays open
to take in the solemn patrons,
the rich shit smell of feedlots
clinging to their dollar bills.

The register rings to the rhythm
of guest checks pierced on a spindle
and the twitch of the driftwood clock.
Red beers all around and the radio
offers the farm market report:

feeder cattle steady to a dollar higher,
soybeans rally at close of day.

And outside, what some people mistake
for empty space exalts its mute palette

while drivers pass through on their way
to Denver, Omaha, or some other
butter and egg route. Whatever you believe
about a place, well, it's going to be true.

Death of the Kapowsin Tavern

I can't ridge it back again from char.
Not one board left. Only ash a cat explores
and shattered glass smoked black and strung
about from the explosion I believe
in the reports. The white school up for sale
for years, most homes abandoned to the rocks
of passing boys—the fire, helped by wind
that blew the neon out six years before,
simply ended lots of ending.

A damn shame. Now, when the night chill
of the lake gets in a troller's bones
where can the troller go for bad wine
washed down frantically with beer?
And when wise men are in style again
will one recount the two-mile glide of cranes
from dead pines or the nameless yellow
flowers thriving in the useless logs,
or dots of light all night about the far end
of the lake, the dawn arrival of the idiot
with catfish—most of all, above the lake
the temple and our sanctuary there?

Nothing dies as slowly as a scene.
The dusty jukebox cracking through
the cackle of a beered-up crone—
wagered wine—sudden need to dance—
these remain in the black debris.
Although I know in time the lake will send
wind black enough to blow it all away.

To the Girl with the Hair at the Club Bar, Troy, MT

You must come here every night
looking for something.
Every night larch burns black in the stove.
The black dog in need of a bath lying down
halfway between the beautiful bar and the door
and the old man, who tries to buy you a drink
each night you see him (every
night), steps over the dog on his way
to his nightly descent.
How you wish the train, raging down
the track on the other side of Yaak Avenue
through the dark, would bring more than
diesel smell and naive hope. Its horn fading
in the hills, like paint fading on this shell
of a bar. Walking seven blocks home
after four Guinness and three games of pool
the stars couldn't be any brighter.

Drinks, Quaffs, and Consumables

"So, while the count stood by the fire, and Paulina Mary still danced to and fro—happy in the liberty of the wide hall-like kitchen—Mrs. Bretton herself instructed Martha to spice and heat the wassail bowl, and, pouring the draught into a Bretton flagon, it was served round, steaming hot, by means of a small silver vessel, which I recognized as Graham's christening cup."

—Charlotte Brontë, *Villette*

The Menu

I beg you come to-night and dine.
A welcome waits you, and sound wine—
The Roederer chilly to a charm,
As Juno's breath the claret warm,
The sherry of an ancient brand.
No Persian pomp, you understand—
A soup, a fish, two meats, and then
A salad fit for aldermen
(When aldermen, alas, the days!
Were really worth their *mayonnaise*);
A dish of grapes whose clusters won
Their bronze in Carolinian sun;
Next, cheese—for you the Neufchâtel,
A bit of Cheshire likes me well;
Café au lait or coffee black,
With Kirsch or Kümmel or Cognac
(The German band in Irving Place
By this time purple in the face);
Cigars and pipes. These being through,
Friends shall drop in, a very few—

Shakespeare and Milton, and no more.
When these are guests I bolt the door,
With Not at Home to any one
Excepting Alfred Tennyson.

Anacreontic to Flip

Stingo! to thy bar-room skip,
Make a foaming mug of Flip;
Make it our country's staple,
Rum New England, Sugar Maple,
Beer, that's brewed from hops and Pumpkin,
Grateful to the thirsty Bumkin.
Hark! I hear thy poker fizzle,
And o'er the mug the liquor drizzle;
All against the earthen mug,
I hear the horn-spoon's cheerful dub;
I see thee, STINGO, take the Flip,
And sling thy cud from under lip,
Then pour more rum, and, bottle stopping,
Stir it again, and swear 'tis topping.
        Come quickly bring the humming liquor,
Richer than ale of British vicar;
Better than usquebaugh Hibernian,
Or than Flaccus' famed Falernian;
More potent, healthy, racy, frisky,
Than Holland's gin, or Georgia whisky.
Come, make a ring around the fire,
And hand the mug unto the Squire;
Here, Deacon, take the elbow chair,

And Ensign, Holiday, sit there:
You take the dye-tub, you the churn,
And I'll the double corner turn.
        See the mantling liquor rise!
And burn their cheeks, and close their eyes,
See the sideling mug incline—
Hear them curse their dull divine,
Who, on Sunday, dared to rail,
At *Brewster's* flip, or *Downer's* ale.
—Quick, Stingo, fly and bring another,
The Deacon here shall pay for t'other,
Ensign and I the third will share,
It's due on swop, for pie-bald mare.

from *Winter*

XXXIX

There underground a magazine
Of sovereign juice is cellar'd in:
Liquor that will the siege maintain,
Should Phoebus ne'er return again.

XL

'Tis that that gives the Poet rage,
And thaws the gelid blood of Age;
Matures the young, restores the old,
And makes the fainting coward bold.

XLI

It lays the careful head to rest,
Calms palpitations in the breast,
Renders our lives' misfortune sweet,
And Venus frolic in the sheet.

XLII

Then let the chill Sirocco blow,
And gird us round with hills of snow;

Or else go whistle to the shore,
And make the hollow mountains roar,

XLIII

Whilst we together jovial sit
Careless, and crown'd with mirth and wit;
Where, though bleak winds confine us home.
Our fancies round the world shall roam.

Whisky, Drink Divine

Whisky, drink divine!
  Why should drivelers bore us
With the praise of wine
  While we've thee before us?
Were it not a shame,
  Whilst we gayly fling thee
To our lips of flame,
  If we could not sing thee?

Greek and Roman sung
  Chian and Falernian—
Shall no harp be strung
  To thy praise, Hibernian?
Yes! let Erin's sons—
  Generous, brave, and frisky—
Tell the world at once
  They owe it to their whisky—

If Anacreon—who
  Was the grape's best poet—
Drank our *mountain-dew,*
  How his verse would show it!
As the best then known,

He to wine was civil;
Had he *Inishowen*,
   He'd pitch wine to the devil—

Bright as beauty's eye,
   When no sorrow veils it:
Sweet as beauty's sigh,
   When young love inhales it:
Come, then, to my lips—
   Come, thou rich in blisses!
Every drop I sip
   Seems a shower of kisses—

Could my feeble lays
   Half thy virtues number,
A whole *grove* of bays
   Should my brows encumber.
Be his name adored,
   Who summed up thy merits
In one little word,
   When we call thee *spirits*—

Send it gayly round—
   Life would be no pleasure,
If we had not found
   This enchanting treasure:

And when tyrant death's
   Arrow shall transfix ye,
Let your latest breaths
   Be whisky! whisky! whisky!

I taste a liquor never brewed

I taste a liquor never brewed,
From tankards scooped in pearl;
Not all the vats upon the Rhine
Yield such an alcohol!

Inebriate of air am I,
And debauchee of dew,
Reeling through endless summer days,
From inns of molten blue.

When landlords turn the drunken bee
Out of the foxglove's door,
When butterflies renounce their drams,
I shall but drink the more!

Till seraphs swing their snowy hats,
And saints to windows run,
To see the little tippler
Leaning against the sun.

Famous Cocktails of New Orleans

    Sazerac

The birthmark on her forehead is a perishing bird.
He hopes to see it on his weeklong layoff.
The woman from the shelter's early reckoning
is in the orchard, cataloguing what a week that was,
charmed by the inside of their experience
into the bloom of an overhearing dry violence
that claims and alms the front pages that finish them.

    Ramos Gin Fizz

In a dead house on the lakefront, first rain begins
and falls over the windows, fracturing the ceramic.
Wearing jeans in the hall, he notices where
she puts her hand as she talks and smells like desert.
He knows his fists and war dead father.
With a bag of clothes he can appear or disappear.
Cross country runners pass in small hours.

    Brandy Milk Punch

Rough cowards put down by the boys last summer
say stay, say stay and don't worry about it,
the damage he has done. One does some damage,
one does some good. At the burning recycling dump

down long road he puts in his application again
and mentally films the branches of live oak
casting shadows on the bread truck's tall sides.

Chartreuse, Neat

She twists the wooden slats for the saddened
arm, serves muffin mix and opened grape.
What do we do about who's calling? This is where
sex leads, these places inside that become the world
and worry and nothing in the Autobiography of
Benjamin Franklin prepares her for the apartment window.
She wakes up and none of it is true. She works.

The Mint Julep

'Tis said that the gods on Olympus of old
   (And who the bright legend profanes with a doubt?)
One night, 'mid their revels, by Bacchus were told
   That his last butt of nectar had somehow run out!

But determined to send round the goblet once more,
   They sued to the fairer immortals for aid
In composing a draught which, till drinking were o'er,
   Should cast every wine ever drank in the shade.

Grave Ceres herself blithely yielded her corn,
   And the spirit that lives in each amber-hued grain,
And which first had its birth from the dew of the morn,
   Was taught to steal out in bright dew-drops again.

Pomona, whose choicest of fruits on the board
   Were scattered profusely in every one's reach,
When called on a tribute to cull from the hoard,
   Expressed the mild juice of the delicate peach.

The liquids were mingled while Venus looked on
　　With glances so fraught with sweet magical power,
That the honey of Hybla, e'en when they were gone,
　　Has never been missed in the draught from that hour.

Flora, then, from her bosom of fragrancy, shook,
　　And with roseate fingers pressed down in the bowl,
All dripping and fresh as it came from the brook,
　　The herb whose aroma should flavor the whole.

The draught was delicious, and loud the acclaim,
　　Though something seemed wanting for all to bewail,
But Juleps the drink of immortals became,
　　When Jove himself added a handful of hail.

A Winter Wish

Old wine to drink!
Ay, give the slippery juice
That drippeth from the grape thrown loose
   Within the tun;
Plucked from beneath the cliff
Of sunny-sided Teneriffe,
  And ripened 'neath the blink
   Of India's sun!
   Peat whiskey hot,
Tempered with well-boiled water!
These make the long night shorter—
   Forgetting not
Good stout old English porter.

Old wood to burn!
Ay, bring the hillside beech
From where the owlets meet and screech,
   And ravens croak;
The crackling pine, and cedar sweet;
Bring, too, a clump of fragrant peat,
  Dug 'neath the fern;
   The knotted oak,
   A fagot too, perhaps,

Whose bright flame, dancing, winking,
Shall light us at our drinking;
    While the oozing sap
Shall make sweet music to our thinking.

  Old books to read!
Ay, bring those nodes of wit,
The brazen-clasped, the vellum writ,
    Time-honored tomes!
The same my sire scanned before,
The same my grandsire thumbed o'er,
The same his sire from college bore,
  The well-earned meed
    Of Oxford's domes:
    Old Homer blind,
Old Horace, rake Anacreon, by
Old Tully, Plautus, Terence lie;
Morte d'Arthur's olden minstrelsie,
Quaint Burton, quainter Spenser, ay!
And Gervase Markham's venerie—
    Nor leave behind
The holye Book by which we live and die.
  Old friends to talk!
Ay, bring those chosen few,
The wise, the courtly, and the true,

So rarely found;
Him for my wine, him for my stud,
Him for my easel, distich, bud
  In mountain walk!
  Bring Walter good,
With soulful Fred, and learned Will,
And thee, my alter ego (dearer still
  For every mood).
These add a bouquet to my wine!
These add a sparkle to my pine!
  If these I tine,
Can books, or fire, or wine be good?

Psalm of Wine and Wind

Here is a sponge filled with wine
And here you are seated upon it.
Pick up your pencil.
They're staring at you.
Tell them you draw the wind
not what's inside it.

A Dithyrambic on Wine

I.

Come! let Mirth our hours employ,
The jolly God inspires;
The rosy juice our bosom fires,
And tunes our souls to joy.
See, great Bacchus now descending,
Gay, with blushing honors crowned;
Sprightly Mirth and Love attending,

Around him wait,
In smiling state—
Let Echo resound
Let Echo resound
The joyful news all around.

II.

Fond Mortals come, if love perplex,
In wine relief you'll find;
Who'd whine for woman's giddy sex
More fickle than the wind?
If beauty's bloom thy fancy warms,
Here see her shine,
Clothed in superior charms;
More lovely than the blushing morn,

When first the opening day
Bedecks the thorn,
And makes the meadows gay.
Here see her in her crystal shrine;
See and adore; confess her all divine,
The Queen of Love and Joy
Heed not thy Chloe's scorn—
    This sparkling glass,
    With winning grace,
Shall ever meet thy fond embrace,
And never, never, never cloy,
    No never, never cloy.

III.
Here, Poet, see, Castalia's spring—
Come, give me a bumper, I'll mount to the skies,
Another, another—'Tis done! I arise;
    On fancy's wing,
    I mount, I sing,
    And now, sublime,
Parnassus' lofty top I climb—
But hark! what sounds are these I hear,
Soft as the dream of her in love,
Or zephyrs whispering through the grove?
And now, more solemn far than funeral woe,

The heavy numbers flow!
    And now again.
    The varied strain,
Grown louder and bolder, strikes quick on the ear,
And thrills through every vein.

IV.
'Tis Pindar's song!
His softer notes the fanning gales
Waft across the spicy vales,
    While through the air,
    Loud whirlwinds bear
The harsher notes along.
    Inspired by wine,
He leaves the lazy crowd below,
Who never dared to peep abroad,
And, mounting to his native sky,
For ever there shall shine.
    No more I'll plod
    The beaten road;
Like him inspired, like him I'll mount high;
    Like his my strain shall flow.

V.

Haste, ye mortals! leave your sorrow;
Let pleasure crown today—tomorrow
    Yield to fate.
Join the universal chorus,
    Bacchus reigns
        Ever great;
    Bacchus reigns
        Ever glorious—
Hark! the joyful groves rebound,
Sporting breezes catch the sound,
And tell to hill and dale around—
    "Bacchus reigns"—
    While far away,
    The busy echoes die away.

Rhenish Night

In my glass, wine trembling like a flame.
I'm listening to the slow song of the boater
recounting seven women under the moon
who unwind green hair down to their feet.

Get up! Sing loud their round dance
to drown out the boater's song
and fill the space around me with
transfixed blondes and their braids.

The Rhine the Rhine gets drunk on the image
of the vineyards on its surface—trembling reflection—
the falling gold of night, groaning song of dying,
green-haired witches who cast the summer's spell—

My glass breaks like a burst of laughter.

—translation by Ed Skoog

The Skirt Story

I hope nature loves the simple tale. The piazza
not overwhelmed by grief, hope, and desire
between sips of a Negroni, and us barely speaking
a language barely understood, sheltered
by umbrellas, the fountain's dorsal pleasure
offsetting heat. After about an hour we'll leave,
roused by clock, or schedule, or need, and go back
to pacing restlessly, stopping only
occasionally. Once, I would have insisted
we want in a way that lets us struggle. Now,
you're trotting down the brick slope
to cross street for ice and water
that should taste awful, through
a troop of husky and pleasant girls and
a donkey? How strange! Within every crowd
there's an exasperated face red as Campari,
someone's teeth sullied with gin, an eye
shaded as if dipped in sweet vermouth, and then
a train's furious bell, a whistle, a hot shimmering
swarm of small violent movements
and you walking, a breath
through masses, skirt breezing around legs.

Grappa in September

The mornings pass clear and deserted
on the river's banks, fogged over by dawn,
their green darkened, awaiting the sun.
In that last house, still damp, at the edge
of the field, they're selling tobacco, blackish,
juicy in flavor: its smoke is pale blue.
They also sell grappa, the color of water.

The moment has come when everything stops
to ripen. The trees in the distance are quiet,
growing darker and darker, concealing fruit
that would fall at a touch. The scattered clouds
are pulpy and ripe. On the distant boulevards,
houses are ripening beneath the mild sky.

This early you see only women. Women don't smoke
and don't drink, they know only to stop in the sun
to let their bodies grow warm, as if they were fruit.
The air's raw with this fog, you drink it in sips
like grappa, everything here has a flavor.
Even the river water has swallowed the banks
and steeps them below, in the sky. The streets
are like women, they grow ripe without moving.

This is the time when each person should pause
in the street to see how everything ripens.
There's even a breeze, it won't move the clouds,
but it's enough to carry the blue smoke along
without breaking it: a new flavor passing. And tobacco
is best when steeped in some grappa. That's why the women
won't be the only ones enjoying the morning.

—translation by Geoffrey Brock

Wassail, Wassail

Wassail, Wassail all over the town!
Our bread it is white and our ale is brown:
Our bowl is made of a maplin tree,
So be my good fellows all—I'll drink to thee.

The wass'ling bowl with a toast within,
Come, fill it up now unto the brim.
Come, fill it up that we may all see,
With the wassailing bowl, I'll drink to thee.

Here's to Dobbin, and to his right ear,
God send our master a happy New Year;
A happy New Year as e'er he did see—
With my Wassailing Bowl I drink to thee.

Here's to Smiler, and to her right eye,
God send our mistress a good Christmas pie;
A good Christmas pie as e'er I did see—
With my Wassailing Bowl I drink to thee.

Here's to Fillpail, and to her long tail,
God send our master us never may fail
Of a cup of good beer; I pray you draw near,
And then you shall hear our jolly Wassail.

And here any maids? I suppose there be some—
Sure they'll not let young men stand on the cold stone;
Sing hey, O maids, come troll back the pin,
And the fairest maid in the house let us all in.

Come, butler, come bring us a bowl of the best,
I hope your soul in Heaven will rest.
But if you do bring us a bowl of the small,
Then down shall go butler, bowl, and all.

Teardrop

Far from the birds, herds, girls
I drank, squatting in some heather
surrounded by a quiet grove of hazel trees
and a misted green afternoon.

What could I drink near the youthful Oise river,
silent elms, grass without flowers, a shuttered sky?
A sip from a gourd fresh off the vine?
A golden liquor to make me pale and sweat.

Like that, I'd turned into a bad sign for a bar.
Then the storm changed sky until evening arrived.
There were dark countries, lakes, poles,
and porches under the blue night, under the stations.

The water from the wood slipped into virgin sands,
the heavenly wind shook ice floes into the ponds . . .
But, like fisherman looking for gold or shells, to think
that I wouldn't want another drink!

—translation by A.J. Rathbun

Describe Divorce to Martinis

Would Jerry Lewis declare the gray sky blue?
Not the heavy telethon host, but the slapstick spasm

for whom you felt pity to give in and laugh.
Would he agree that even the ugliest scars grow smooth,

become bearable hours in an empty house, the answer
to where does your son sometimes sleep?

Ask the comedians where laughter ends up living after the split,
the meaning of a pocketful of toothpicks and olives;

ask them to repeatedly perform their slapstick routines
until the universe is shaken and stirred

into a tolerable concoction that seems suave
and smooth but burns the gut like swallowed bleach.

Better yet, ask Jerry to rise from some farcical flop on the floor
and pour another drink for Dean, staggering Dean, charming Dino

slurring each syllable as if no sound should ever be alone. In fact,
make it two. I'll have whatever the guy in the tux is drinking.

Ceremony

I followed him into the streets of his youth
to the raucous corner of 7th and 57th,
where, in a sly ceremony,
he opened a violin case on the sidewalk

and removed a bottle of gin,
a bottle of vermouth, still sealed,
a jar of green olives, pitted but not stuffed,
and a small tin of square toothpicks.

He performed
without the aid of ice, shaker or glassware,
filling his mouth directly
as he gargled a song

and made broad flourishes with his arms.

§

Martini containing a rain shower
soaking the white shirt
of a man pressing his hands to his face.

A Twist-imony in Favor of Gin-Twist

1.

At one in the morn, as I went staggering home,
  With nothing at all in my hand but my fist,
At the end of the street a good youth I did meet,
  Who asked me to join in a jug of gin-twist.

2.

"Though 'tis late," I replied, "and I'm muggy beside,
  Yet an offer like this I could never resist;
So let's waddle away, *sans* a moment's delay,
  And in style we'll demolish your jug of gin-twist."

3.

The friends of the grape may boast of rich Cape,
  Hock, Claret, Madeira, or Lachryma Christ,
But this muzzle of mine was never so fine
  As to value them more than a jug of gin-twist.

4.

The people of Nantz, in the kingdom of France,
  Bright brandy they brew, liquor not to be hissed;
It may do as a dram, but 'tis not worth a damn,
  When watered, compared with a jug of gin-twist.

5.

Antigua, Jamaica, they certainly make a
   Grand species of rum, which should ne'er be dismissed;
It is splendid as grog, but never, you dog,
   Esteem it as punch, like a jug of gin-twist.

6.

Ye bailies of Glasgow! Wise men of the West!
   Without your rum bowls you'd look certainly *tristes;*
Yet I laugh when I'm told that liquor so cold
   Is as good as a foaming hot jug of gin-twist.

7.

The bog-trotting Teagues in clear whisky delight,
   Preferring potsheen to all drinks that exist;
I grieve, ne'ertheless, that it does not possess
   The juniper smack of a jug of gin-twist.

8.

Farintosh and Glenlivet, I hear, are the boast
   Of those breechesless heroes, the Sons of the Mist;
But may I go choke if that villainous smoke
   I'd name in a day with a jug of gin-twist.

9.

Yet the Celtic I love, and should join them, by Jove!
    Though Glengarry should vow I'd no right to enlist;
For that chief, do you see, I'd not care a bawbee,
    If strongly entrenched o'er a jug of gin-twist.

10.

One rule they lay down is the reason, I own,
    Why from joining their plaided array I desist;
Because they declare that no one shall wear
    Of breeches a pair, o'er their jugs of gin-twist.

11.

This is plainly absurd, I give you my word,
    Of this bare-rumped reg'lation I ne'er saw the gist;
In my gay corduroys, can't these philabeg boys
    Suffer me to get drunk o'er my jug of gin-twist?

12.

In India they smack a liquor called rack,
    Which I never quaffed (at least that I wist);
I'm told 'tis like tow in its taste, and, if so,
    Very different stuff from a jug of gin-twist.

13.

As for porter and ale—'fore Gad, I turn pale,
    When people on such things as these can insist;
They may do for dull clods, but, by all of the gods!
    They are hog-wash when matched with a jug of gin-twist.

14.

Why tea we import I could never conceive;
    To the Mandarin folk, to be sure, it brings grist;
But in our western soils the spirits it spoils,
    While to heaven they are raised by a jug of gin-twist.

15.

Look at Hazlitt and Hunt, most unfortunate pair!
    Black and blue from the kicks of a stern satirist;
But would Mynheer Izzard once trouble their gizzard,
    If bohea they exchanged for a jug of gin-twist?

16.

Leibnitz held that this earth was the first of all worlds,
    And no wonder the buck was a firm optimist;
For 'twas always his use, as a proof to adduce
    Of the truth of his doctrine, a jug of gin-twist.

17.

It cures all the vapours and mulligrub capers;

    It makes you like Howard, the philanthro-pist;

Woe, trouble, and pain, that bother your brain,

    Are banished out clean by a jug of gin-twist.

18.

You turn up your nose at all of your foes,

    Abuse you, traduce you, they may if they list;

The lawyers, I'm sure, would look very poor,

    If their clients would stick to their jugs of gin-twist.

19.

There's Leslie, my friend, who went ramstam to law,

    Because Petre had styled him a poor Hebraist;

And you see how the jury, in spite of his fury,

    Gave him comfort far less than one jug of gin-twist.

20.

And therefore, I guess, sir, the *celebre* Professor,

    Even though culpably quizzed as a mere sciolist,

Would have found it much neater to have laughed at old Petre,

    And got drunk with Kit North o'er a jug of gin-twist.

21.

Its medical virtues * * * *

* * * * * * * * * *

* * * * * * * * * *

* * * * a jug of gin-twist.

22.

By its magical aid a toper is made,

    Like Brockden Brown's hero, a ventriloquist;

For my belly cries out, with an audible shout,

    "Fill up every chink with a jug of gin-twist."

23.

Geologers all, great, middling, and small,

    Whether fiery Plutonian or wet Neptunist,

Most gladly, it seems, seek proofs for their schemes

    In the water, or spirit, of a jug of gin-twist.

24.

These grubbers of ground (whom God may confound!),

    Forgetting transition, trap, hornblende, or schist,

And all other sorts, think only of quartz—

    I mean, of the quarts in a jug of gin-twist.

25.

Though two dozen of verse I've contrived to rehearse,
   Yet still I can sing like a true melodist;
For they are but asses who think that Parnassus
   In spirit surpasses a jug of gin-twist.

26.

It makes you to speak Dutch, Latin, or Greek;
   Even learning Chinese very much 'twould assist:
I'll discourse you in Hebrew, provided that ye brew
   A most Massorethical jug of gin-twist.

27.

When its amiable stream, all enveloped in steam,
   Is dashed to and fro by a vigorous wrist,
How sweet a cascade every moment is made
   By the artist who fashions a jug of gin-twist!

28.

Sweet stream! There is none but delights in thy flow,
   Save that vagabond villain, the Whig atheist;
For done was the job for his patron, Sir Bob,
   When he dared to wage war 'gainst a jug of gin-twist.

29.

Don't think by its name, from Geneva it came,
    The sour little source of the Kirk Calvinist—
A fig for Jack Calvin! My processes alvine
    Are much more rejoiced by a jug of gin-twist.

30.

Let the *Scotsman* delight in malice and spite,
    The black-legs at Brooks's in hazard or whist;
Tom Dibdin in books, Micky Taylor in cooks:
    My pleasure is fixed in a jug of gin-twist.

31.

Though the point of my nose grow as red as a rose
    Or rival in hue a superb amethyst,
Yet no matter for that, I tell you *'tis* flat,
    I shall still take a pull at a jug of gin-twist.

32.

There was old Cleobulus, who, meaning to fool us,
    Gave out for his saying, ΤΟ ΜΕΤΡΟΝ ΑΡΙΣΤ;
But he'd never keep measure, if he had but the pleasure
    Of washing his throat with a jug of gin-twist.

33.

There are dandies and blockheads, who vapour and boast
    Of the favours of girls they never have kissed;
That is not the thing, and therefore, by jing!
    I kiss while I'm praising my jug of gin-twist.

34.

While over the glass I should be an ass
    To make moping love like a dull Platonist;
That ne'er was my fashion: I swear that my passion
    Is as hot as itself for a jug of gin-twist.

35.

Although it is time to finish my rhyme,
    Yet the subject's so sweet I can scarcely desist;
While its grateful perfume is delighting the room,
    How can I be mute o'er a jug of gin-twist?

36.

Yet since I've made out, without any doubt,
    Of its merits and glories a flourishing list,
Let us end with a toast, which we cherish the most:
    Here's "God save the King!" in a glass of gin-twist.

37.
Then I bade him good-night in a most jolly plight,
But I'm sorry to say that my footing I missed;
All the stairs I fell down, so I battered my crown,
And got two black eyes from a jug of gin-twist.

Drinkers, Revelers, and Imbibers

"The gentleman in his cups is a gentleman always, and the man who tells his friend in his cups that he is in love does so because the fact has been very present to himself in his cooler and calmer moments."

— Anthony Trollope, *He Knew He Was Right*

Reasons for Drinking

If all be true that I do think,
There are five reasons we should drink;
Good wine—a friend—or being dry—
Or lest we should be by and by—
Or any other reason why.

The Toper's Rant

Come, come, my old crones and gay fellows
That love to drink ale in a horn,
We'll sing racy songs now we're mellow
Which topers sung ere we were born.

For our bottle kind fate shall be thanked,
And line but our pockets with brass,
We'll sooner suck ale through a blanket
Than thimbles of wine from a glass.

Away with your proud thimble glasses
Of wine foreign nations supply,
We topers ne'er drink to the lasses
Over draughts scarce enough for a fly.

Club us with the hedger and ditcher
Or beggar that makes his own horn,
To join us o'er bottle or pitcher
Foaming o'er with the essence of corn.

We care not with whom we get tipsy
Or where with brown stout we regale,
We'll weather the storm with a gipsy
If he be a lover of ale.

We'll weather the toughest storm weary
Although we get wet to the skin,
If outside our cottage looks dreary
We're warm and right happy within.

We'll sit till the bushes are dropping
Like the spout of a watering-pan,
For till the dram's drank there's no stopping,
We'll keep up the ring to a man.

We'll sit till Dame Nature is feeling
The breath of our stingo so warm,
And bushes and trees begin reeling
In our eyes like to ships in a storm.

We'll sit for three hours before seven,
When larks wake the morning to dance,
Till night's sooty brood of eleven,
With witches ride over to France.

We'll sit it in spite of the weather
Till we tumble our length on the plain,
When the morning shall find us together,
To play the game over again.

Poem 27

Are you tending the bar, kid? Pour me the strong stuff,
the Falernian wine, and one for yourself. We're going to need it,
the way this party is going. Our host, Postumia, is drunker than
these grapes. No water, please. It kills what wine is.
Save water for the fool who prefers his own sorrow.
This wine is more than wine. It's the blood of the god
whose mother was destroyed by his father's splendor,
the god of madness and ecstasy, who shares it with us.

—translation by Ed Skoog

To Live Merrily,
and to Trust to Good Verses

Now is the time for mirth,
    Nor cheek or tongue be dumb;
For, with the flow'ry earth,
    The golden pomp is come.

The golden pomp is come;
    For now each tree does wear,
Made of her pap and gum,
    Rich beads of amber here.

Now reigns the rose, and now
    Th' Arabian dew besmears
My uncontrolled brow
    And my retorted hairs.

Homer, this health to thee,
    In sack of such a kind
That it would make thee see
    Though thou wert ne'er so blind.

Next, Virgil I'll call forth
   To pledge this second health
In wine, whose each cup's worth
   An Indian commonwealth.

A goblet next I'll drink
   To Ovid, and suppose,
Made he the pledge, he'd think
   The world had all one nose.

Then this immensive cup
   Of aromatic wine,
Catullus, I quaff up
   To that terse muse of thine.

Wild I am now with heat:
   O Bacchus! cool thy rays!
Or, frantic, I shall eat
   Thy thyrse, and bite the bays.

Round, round the roof does run;
   And, being ravished thus,
Come, I will drink a tun
   To my Propertius.

Now, to Tibullus, next,
   This flood I drink to thee;
But stay, I see a text
   That this presents to me.

Behold, Tibullus lies
   Here burnt, whose small return
Of ashes scarce suffice
   To fill a little urn.

Trust to good verses, then;
   They only will aspire
When pyramids, as men,
   Are lost i' th' funeral fire.

And when all bodies meet
   In Lethe to be drowned,
Then only numbers sweet
   With endless life are crowned.

Oh, For a Bowl of Fat Canary

Oh, for a bowl of fat Canary,
Rich Palermo, sparkling Sherry,
Some nectar else, from Juno's dairy;
Oh, these draughts would make us merry!

Oh, for a wench (I deal in faces,
And in other daintier things);
Tickled am I with her embraces,
Fine dancing in such fairy rings.

Oh, for a plump fat leg of mutton,
Veal, lamb, capon, pig, and coney;
None is happy but a glutton,
None an ass but who wants money.

Wines indeed and girls are good,
But brave victuals feast the blood;
For wenches, wine, and lusty cheer,
Jove would leap down to surfeit here.

On Lending a Punch Bowl

This ancient silver bowl of mine,—it tells of good old times,
Of joyous days, and jolly nights, and merry Christmas chimes;
They were a free and jovial race, but honest, brave, and true,
That dipped their ladle in the punch when this old bowl was new.

A Spanish galleon brought the bar,—so runs the ancient tale;
'Twas hammered by an Antwerp smith, whose arm was like a flail;
And now and then between the strokes, for fear his strength
    should fail,
He wiped his brow, and quaffed a cup of good old Flemish ale.

'Twas purchased by an English squire to please his loving dame,
Who saw the cherubs, and conceived a longing for the same;
And oft as on the ancient stock another twig was found,
'Twas filled with caudle spiced and hot, and handed smoking
    round.

But, changing hands, it reached at length a Puritan divine,
Who used to follow Timothy, and take a little wine,
But hated punch and prelacy; and so it was, perhaps,
He went to Leyden, where he found conventicles and schnapps.

And then, of course, you know what's next,—it left the Dutchman's
    shore
With those that in the Mayflower came,—a hundred souls and
    more,—
Along with all the furniture, to fill their new abodes,—
To judge by what is still on hand, at least a hundred loads.

'Twas on a dreary winter's eve, the night was closing dim,
When brave Miles Standish took the bowl, and filled it to the brim;
The little Captain stood and stirred the posset with his sword,
And all his sturdy men-at-arms were ranged about the board.

He poured the fiery Hollands in,—the man that never feared,—
He took a long and solemn draught, and wiped his yellow beard;
And one by one the musketeers—the men that fought and prayed—
All drank as 'twere their mother's milk, and not a man afraid.

That night, affrighted from his nest, the screaming eagle flew,
He heard the Pequot's ringing whoop, the soldier's wild halloo;
And there the sachem learned the rule he taught to kith and kin,
"Run from the white man when you find he smells of Hollands gin!"

A hundred years, and fifty more, had spread their leaves and
    snows,
A thousand rubs had flattened down each little cherub's nose,

When once again the bowl was filled, but not in mirth or joy,
'Twas mingled by a mother's hand to cheer her parting boy.

"Drink, John," she said, "'t will do you good,—poor child, you'll
     never bear
This working in the dismal trench, out in the midnight air;
And if—God bless me!—you were hurt, 'twould keep away the chill."
So John *did* drink,—and well he wrought that night at Bunker's Hill!

I tell you, there was generous warmth in good old English cheer
I tell you, 'twas a pleasant thought to bring its symbol here.
'Tis but the fool that loves excess;—hast thou a drunken soul?
Thy bane is in thy shallow skull, not in my silver bowl!

I love the memory of the past,—its pressed yet fragrant flowers,—
The moss that clothes its broken walls,—the ivy on its towers;—
Nay, this poor bauble it bequeathed,—my eyes grow moist and dim,
To think of all the vanished joys that danced around its brim.

Then fill a fair and honest cup, and bear it straight to me;
The goblet hallows all it holds, whate'er the liquid be;
And may the cherubs on its face protect me from the sin
That dooms one to those dreadful words,— "My dear, where *have*
     you been?"

Cocktail Music

All my life a brook of voices
has run in my ears,
many separate instruments
tuning and playing, tuning.
It's cocktail music,
the sound of my parents
in their thirties,
glass-lined ice bucket loaded
and reloaded but no one tending bar,
little paper napkins, cigarettes,
kids passing hors d'oeuvres.
It's drinking music,
riffle of water over stones,
ice in glasses, rise and fall
of many voices touching—
that music. Husbands grilling meat,
squirting the fire to keep it down,
a joke erupting, bird voices snipping
at something secret by the bar.
It's all the voices collapsed
into one voice,
urgent and muscled like a river
then lowered as in a drought,

but never gone. It's the background.
When I lift the shell to my ear
it's in there.

The Parting Glass

The man that joins in life's career
And hopes to find some comfort here,
To rise above this earthly mass,—
The only way's to drink his glass.

But still, on this uncertain stage
Where hopes and fears the soul engage,
And while, amid the joyous band,
Unheeded flows the measured sand,
Forget not as the moments pass
That time shall bring the parting glass!

In spite of all the mirth I've heard,
This is the glass I always feared,
The glass that would the rest destroy,
The farewell cup, the close of joy!

With you, whom reason taught to think,
I could for ages sit and drink;
But with the fool, the sot, the ass,
I haste to take the parting glass.

The luckless wight, that still delays
His draught of joys to future days,

Delays too long—for then, alas!
Old age steps up, and—breaks the glass!

The nymph who boasts no borrowed charms,
Whose sprightly wit my fancy warms,—
What though she tends this country inn,
And mixes wine, and deals out gin?
With such a kind, obliging lass,
I sigh to take the parting glass.

With him who always talks of gain
(Dull Momus, of the plodding train),
The wretch who thrives by others' woes,
And carries grief where'er he goes,—
With people of this knavish class
The first is still my parting glass.

With those that drink before they dine,
With him that apes the grunting swine,
Who fills his page with low abuse,
And strives to act the gabbling goose
Turned out by fate to feed on grass—
Boy, give me quick, the parting glass.

The man whose friendship is sincere,
Who knows no guilt, and feels no fear,—

It would require a heart of brass
With him to take the parting glass!

With him who quaffs his pot of ale,
Who holds to all an even scale,
Who hates a knave in each disguise,
And fears him not—whate'er his size—
With him, well pleased my days to pass,
May Heaven forbid the Parting Glass!

Climb Up

The wild wind, the expressing sky, the ape's pained cry,
and on the distant island, birds circle over white sand.
Continually, the trees let go of leaf, leaf, leaf.
The river's impulses are a wave repeating after a wave.
I've moved ten thousand autumn miles to be solely a guest,
shouldered a hundred years of disease, and now climb
to the stage. Alone, I hate the gray hair at my temples—
but my biggest disappointment? I forgot my glass of fortified wine.

—*translation by A.J. Rathbun*

With an Honest Old Friend

With an honest old friend and a merry old song,
And a flask of old Port let me sit the night long,
And laugh at the malice of those who repine
That they must drink porter, whilst I can drink wine.

I envy no mortal tho' ever so great,
Nor scorn I a wretch for his lowly estate;
But what I abhor and esteem as a curse,
Is poorness of spirit, not poorness of purse.

Then dare to be generous, dauntless and gay,
Let's merrily pass life's remainder away;
Upheld by our friends, we our foes may despise,
For the more we are envied, the higher we rise.

J. ROBERT LENNON

Drinking Song

I nursed my drink
but it couldn't be saved.
Unshaven, cursed,
I got right to work
on its doomed replacement.

My table was strewn
with tombstones of glass.
Mass murderer, I
fell face down on their graves
and declared myself sated.

But a strange thing occurs
at a quarter to two,
when the neon moon shakes
the dead from their rest
and wrestles the ghouls

from the swamp of the floor
to the stumps of their stools.
Drooling, I swore
I would murder again!
Ignominious fools

with their rules
and locked doors!
I demanded a brace
of martinis and fizzes,
called waitresses whores

and bartenders
pissants, then drained
every glass with artless
abandon. The rest
was a blur. Restrained,

ejected, I found
myself on the street,
beaten and naked,
clutching the curb
with hands like raw meat.

The battle was won.
I screamed for my bottle
as daylight delivered
the glint of hot metal.
But the drinks didn't come.

Both Portraits

In his bleary memory she poses
like an immaculate mannequin,
her eyes pimentos, joints frozen
in a gesture he's grown to know.

Loss is like a bluebottle fly
buzzing around in a mug of bourbon.
She'll come back. Any minute,
he keeps telling himself.

One day pours into the next
but he can still see her.
A dark square nailed to the wall.
A portrait taken down for good.

Drunk Last Night With Friends, I Go To Work Anyway

The boss knows what shape I'm in. He tells me
about the twenties, when he was my age,
how he drank all night and woke up in strange rooms
with strange dolls. He tells me *Get lost.*

Out back, a weedbank I'd never noticed—
I head for it in cold air, remembering
dogs and cats eating grass when sick.

I sit shoulder deep in weeds. Beneath the leaves
in green air, black beetles shoulder
enormous stems, dew quivering
between stalk and leaf. In the pale moss I see
ants the size of salt grains,
and budding red flowers
smaller than these ants. A snail
dreaming in the throat of an old wine bottle.

The Mamelukes May Love

The Mamelukes may love
their Nile waters, the Spanish
may swear by the raging
Tagus river, but I will not
be sucked in to sipping this weak wetness.
And if ever one of my friends
dips a single finger into these deeps,
I'll strangle them with my own hands.
Let the quacks and quaking go pluck
lean lettuces, herbs, and chicory
to mix with water and rid
them of evil thoughts.
My friends and I skip
the spigots of plain water, even
banish watered Limoncello
from our parties. Sweet ladies,
for a moment, do not drink,
but run your fingers like garlands
through my hair. I won't crave your
sugary egg punch, or golden
sorbets, a thousand fragranced waters,
because these indolent drinks are only

for your sweet lips. Wine, wine
is for those that desire euphoria,
to forget their fears. But be not shy about it—
I tip my glasses crazily, happily,
at least six times a year.

—translation by A.J. Rathbun

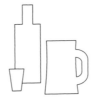

I was Drunk on the Beach in Oaxaca

Oaxaca?

Oaxaca. It was dawn. The darkness was still glued to the horizon
by a squeeze of light. Cruise ships lifted anchors and curved out of
sight. My eyes would not close. They were like the all night liquor
store on the corner of Steiner and Hyde.

Steiner? In Oaxaca?

Yes. Oaxaca. I was open all night. My heart slid open and closed
like a freezer full of popsicles.

I'm sorry. Are we talking about the same town? Oaxaca for lovers?

Oaxaca for Julie and Jason.

And you were able to get drunk there? Impossible.

But I was looking east. Sun was coming at me like a church bus.
I was standing by the ocean.

So, you were drunk on the beach in Oaxaca.

Yes, I was standing on the beach in Oaxaca, hammered, when I realized I'd gone and done it again.

Yes, but did you see the water?

It was too dark to say, but I sensed its presence. I smelled the plankton. I heard the echoing snap of a pelican beak.

Drinking Alone by Moonlight

I drag my wine jug where the flowers are
to drink without my friends or their love.
I toast the moon, invite it down to join
my shadow and I, so there will be three of us,
but the moon doesn't drink and drive,
and my shadow will only follow behind.
Still, the moon travels with us.
It *has* to. Spring is almost summer.

I croon, and the moon's a crooner,
I boogie, and my shadow boogaloos.
We get along so well when we're sober.
Tonight, drunk, we're falling into disarray.
Hey guys, next time let's do our strange
inhuman drinking on the shore of the river of stars.

—translation by Ed Skoog

Aging

I tasted and spat
as the experts did
so I could taste again.
I put my nose in. I cleansed
my palate with bread.
A friend guided me;
he thought because I drank often
I drank well.
He thought I might be looking
for subtleties, as he was.
My vocabulary was "good"
and "not so good."
Usually I was a drinker
looking for a mood.
We moved among the oak barrels
and private reserves,
the fine talk of the serious
performing their delicate
mysterious craft.
Yet about the art of aging
I found myself indifferent,
nothing to say or ask.
We went outside,

walked among the woody vines
and fleshy, often violet,
sometimes green, prodigal,
smooth-skinned grapes.
The day was beautiful.
My friend was happy, sated.
There's never enough, I thought.
There can never be enough.

A.J. RATHBUN is a food and entertaining writer and poet and the author of the poetry collection *Want* (a ZYZZYVA First Book), as well as eight cookbooks, including *Good Spirits* (winner of an IACP Cookbook award), *Dark Spirits*, *Champagne Cocktails*, and *Double Take* (coauthored with Jeremy Holt). He has published poetry in the magazines *Crazyhorse, Gulf Coast, The Sonora Review, The Southeast Review, Third Coast, Weber Studies, Willow Springs*, and *ZYZZYVA*, is a frequent guest on the Everyday Food program (Martha Stewart Living / Sirius satellite radio), and is a contributor to many culinary and entertaining magazines, including *Every Day with Rachael Ray, The Food Network Magazine, Real Simple, Eating Well,* and *Wine Enthusiast*. He is a member of the International Association of Culinary Professionals and the Museum of the American Cocktail and for years was the co-publisher and editor of the Seattle literary magazine *LitRag*. A.J. lives in Seattle, and invites you to visit his website, www.ajrathbun.com, where you can read his blog, Spiked Punch.